Classic Collection

PINOCCHIO

CARLO COLLODI

Adapted by Ronne Randall • Illustrated by Claudia Venturini

QEB Publishing

A Boy Made of Wood

Geppetto was a lonely old woodcarver who longed to have a son. One day, his friend Antonio gave him a very special piece of wood, and Geppetto decided he would make a puppet out of it.

"It will be a wonderful puppet," he told Antonio, "one that can dance, fence, turn somersaults…almost like a real boy!"

Geppetto started carving the wood. "I will name this puppet Pinocchio," he told himself. "I once knew a man named Pinocchio, and he was very lucky. This puppet will bring me good luck and be like a real son."

As soon as he had carved Pinocchio's head, the nose began to grow! The more Geppetto tried to shorten it, the longer it grew! And to his surprise, when he carved Pinocchio's mouth, the puppet laughed at him.

Geppetto managed to carve Pinocchio's body and arms and then his legs. But as soon as Geppetto had carved his feet, Pinocchio kicked him and ran outside!

Geppetto ran after Pinocchio. "Catch him! Catch him!" he shouted to the people in the street.

"No!" cried Pinocchio. "Please save me from that cruel man!" And he ran faster.

A policeman nearby heard the shouting, and when he saw Pinocchio running away from the old man, he grabbed Geppetto.

"Being cruel to a helpless puppet, are you?" he said, and he took Geppetto straight to prison!

The Talking Cricket

Pinocchio ran back home, closed the door, and breathed a sigh of relief. Suddenly, a strange chirping noise made him turn around: "Crick-crick. Crick-crick!"

"Who's there?" Pinocchio asked, frightened.

"It's me, the Talking Cricket."

Pinocchio saw a big green cricket climbing up the wall. "What do you want, you ugly bug?" he asked.

"I want to help you," the Cricket said kindly, "by telling you something very important: children who disobey their parents and run away will never be happy. Happy children go to school and study or learn a trade so that they can make their way in the world."

"I don't care!" Pinocchio shouted. "I don't want to go to school, or work, or do anything except eat and drink and play. And that's exactly what I *will* do!"

"You will be sorry," said the Cricket.

"And I think *you're* the one who will be sorry!" said Pinocchio, picking up one of Geppetto's tools and running after the Cricket, who luckily managed to escape through an open window.

Pinocchio lay down to rest, but he was too hungry to sleep. He got up and searched the house. There was not a single crumb to be found anywhere.

"Maybe that Cricket was right," thought Pinocchio sadly. "If I hadn't run away, Father would be here now—and I wouldn't be hungry. Poor me!"

Pinocchio was so tired that he fell asleep. At dawn, he awoke to hear Geppetto coming in.

"I'm sorry I ran away!" Pinocchio sobbed. "I am so hungry, Father. I promise I will never be naughty again!"

Geppetto had been angry with Pinocchio, but hearing the puppet cry softened his heart. He took three fat, juicy pears out of his pocket and gave them to Pinocchio.

"These were going to be my breakfast," he said, "but I am happy to give them to you."

Pinocchio gobbled up all three pears. Geppetto, of course, had no breakfast at all.

After his meal, Pinocchio was in a much better mood. When Geppetto told him that he would have to go to school, just like a real boy, Pinocchio agreed.

"Of course, I will need some clothes, Father," he said, "and an ABC book."

"Yes, you will," said Geppetto. As he had no money, he made Pinocchio a suit of flowered paper, a hat made of dough, and little wooden shoes. "You look like a real gentleman now!" he said proudly.

Then Geppetto took his only coat and left the house. He came back shivering, wearing just his shirt.

"Where is your coat, Father?" Pinocchio asked.

"I sold it," Geppetto replied, "to buy you this." And he held out a brand-new ABC book.

"Now you are ready for school!" he said happily, handing the book to Pinocchio.

The Puppet Theater

Pinocchio set off for school, proudly carrying his new ABC book under his arm. He was thinking about how much he would learn, when he heard the sound of music in the distance. Curious, he stopped to listen.

"I know I should go to school," he said to himself, "but I can do that later. Right now, I'll see where the music is coming from!" And off he ran, straight to the town square.

A brightly colored tent, with a sign saying "Puppet Theater," stood in the middle of the square.

"How much does it cost to get in?" Pinocchio asked a man at the entrance.

"Four cents," the man replied.

"I don't have any money," Pinocchio said, "but here's my ABC book!" The man took it and let him in.

Inside, Pinocchio could not believe his eyes. Wooden puppets just like him were on the stage performing! The people watching them were laughing and clapping.

Suddenly, one of the puppets onstage stopped and pointed at Pinocchio.

"Look!" she shouted. "One of our wooden brothers has come to see us!"

"Yes!" cried another puppet. "Come up and join us!"

Pinocchio leaped onto the stage, and the audience cheered wildly. He spent the rest of the day singing and dancing with the other puppets. In all of the fun, Pinocchio forgot about the promise he had made to Geppetto.

The Fox and the Cat

When the show was over, the Puppeteer, Pinocchio, and the other puppets ate a delicious meal together and then danced until the sun came up. Before he left, the Puppeteer gave Pinocchio five gold coins for Geppetto.

Pinocchio meant to go straight home—really, he did. But on his way, he met a lame fox and a blind cat, who stopped to talk to him.

"Good morning, Pinocchio," said the Fox.

"How do you know my name?" Pinocchio asked.

"We know your father, Geppetto, well," the Fox replied. "We saw him just this morning, shivering in his shirtsleeves."

"He won't be shivering much longer," Pinocchio said. "I have five gold pieces, so I can buy a new coat for Father and a new ABC book for myself. I will go to school and make Father proud of me."

"Listen," said the Cat. "We know how you can turn those five gold pieces into thousands!"

"How?" Pinocchio asked.

"We can take you to a place called the Field of Wonders," the Fox explained. "There, you just have to bury a gold piece under a tree, water it, and leave it overnight. In the morning, one gold piece will have turned into five hundred!"

Pinocchio could not resist. "All right," he said. "I will come with you."

The Cricket's Warning

It was a long way to the Field of Wonders. After walking most of the day, Pinocchio and his new friends stopped at an inn for dinner.

"We will start out again at midnight," said the Fox, "and we will get to the Field of Wonders by dawn."

After dinner, the Fox asked the innkeeper for two rooms so that they could rest before continuing their journey. The Fox and the Cat took one room, and Pinocchio took the other. As soon as he was in bed, he fell fast asleep.

When he woke up, he found that the Fox and the Cat had left without him—and without paying the innkeeper! Pinocchio had to use one of his gold coins to pay for their dinner and rooms.

He set out on his own, hoping he could still find the Field of Wonders. A little way down the road, he saw a green glow in a tree. As he got closer, he realized it was the Talking Cricket!

"Don't trust those two swindlers," said the Cricket. "Go home to your father."

"I will go home to Father," said Pinocchio, "but only when I am rich. I have to find the Field of Wonders first."

"The night is very dark, and the road is full of danger," the Cricket warned.

"I don't care," said Pinocchio. "I'm going on, no matter what you say. I'm going to make Father rich!"

"Be careful, Pinocchio!" the Cricket called after him. "You may be sorry!"

Pinocchio continued down the road, muttering to himself about how annoying the Talking Cricket was. "All he ever does is scold me and tell me what to do," he said to himself. "Once I've made my fortune, he'll see how wrong he was!"

Suddenly, just ahead, he saw two shadowy figures wrapped in black cloaks. He tried to run, but they were too quick for him. Grabbing his arms, they growled, "Give us your money!"

Wiggling and twisting, Pinocchio managed to bite one of the robbers on the hand—but it felt like a paw to him! Screaming with pain, the thief let him go, and Pinocchio fled through the woods.

His attackers followed him, and at last they caught up. Whipping out a piece of rope, they hung him from the branch of a tall oak tree.

"We'll be back in the morning," they told him. "By that time, maybe you will change your mind about giving us your money!"

Poor Pinocchio! He was cold, tired, and frightened. He was sure that the robbers would kill him when they came back.

"Father!" he wailed. "If only you could help me!"

Pinocchio didn't know it, but in a cottage nearby there lived a kind and gentle Fairy with Blue Hair.

She heard Pinocchio's cries, and her heart was filled with pity for him.

The Fairy with Blue Hair

The lovely Fairy with Blue Hair called for her falcon and told him to fly to Pinocchio and take him down from the tree. Then she sent her golden coach into the forest to bring Pinocchio back to her.

The coach, pulled by two hundred white mice, returned quickly, and the Fairy brought Pinocchio into her cottage. He was more dead than alive by now, so the Fairy summoned three doctors to examine him—the Crow, the Owl, and the Talking Cricket.

"Can he be saved?" she asked each of them.

"No," said the Crow. "He is dead and gone."

Then the Owl stepped forward. "I am sorry to disagree," he said, "but this puppet is alive!"

"What do you think?" the Fairy asked the Talking Cricket.

"I have known this puppet for a long time," said the Cricket, "and I know that he is rude and lazy and a runaway."

Although Pinocchio's eyes were still closed, he shuddered at the Cricket's words.

"He is a disobedient son," the Talking Cricket continued, "and he has broken his father's heart!"

When he heard this, Pinocchio began to cry loudly. Tears streamed down his wooden face.

"When the dead weep," said the Crow, "it is a sure sign that they are beginning to recover."

The Fairy thanked all three doctors, and they left.

Pinocchio's Nose Grows!

The Fairy gave Pinocchio some medicine, and very soon he felt better. She asked how he had come to be dangling from a tree branch.

Pinocchio told her about the five gold coins, about the Fox and the Cat and the Field of Wonders, and about meeting the cloaked robbers in the forest.

"Where are your gold coins now?" she asked.

"I…I lost them," said Pinocchio, even though they were in his pocket. As soon as he told this lie, Pinocchio's nose began to grow.

"Where did you lose them?" asked the Fairy.

"Ummm…in the forest," said Pinocchio. His nose grew even longer! The Fairy began to laugh.

"Why are you laughing?" Pinocchio asked.

"I am laughing," said the Fairy, "because with every lie you tell, your nose grows longer."

Pinocchio was so upset that he tried to run away, but his nose was too long to fit through the door. He sat down and sobbed. Feeling sorry for Pinocchio, the Fairy sent for a flock of woodpeckers. They pecked at his nose until it was back to its normal size.

"You are so good to me, kind Fairy," Pinocchio said. "I never want to leave!"

"And I wish you could stay here with me, too," said the Fairy, "but your father is on his way to fetch you."

So Pinocchio ran off to meet him.

Pinocchio had not gotten very far when he met the Fox and the Cat. "What are you doing here?" they asked.

Pinocchio told them about the robbers who had tried to steal his gold.

"Terrible rascals!" said the Fox.

"Shocking!" said the Cat. "What happened to your gold pieces?"

"I still have them," said Pinocchio.

"Excellent!" said the Fox. "Then you can still bury them in the Field of Wonders! We'll take you there now."

They walked for hours, until they came to a lonely field. There Pinocchio dug a hole and carefully buried his four gold pieces. He sprinkled the soil with water.

"Now," said the Fox, "go away for twenty minutes. When you come back, a vine will have sprung up, with gold coins hanging from it."

"Thank you!" said Pinocchio. He skipped away happily, thinking about the riches he would soon have.

But when he came back, the Cat and the Fox were gone, and there was no vine—just an empty hole in the ground where his coins had been.

"Ha-ha-ha-ha!" On a nearby tree, a parrot sat and laughed as he groomed his bright feathers.

"What are you laughing at?" asked Pinocchio.

"I am laughing at a silly boy who lets himself be fooled by scoundrels!" said the Parrot.

Pinocchio knew the bird was right. Now he had nothing at all, and it was his own fault.

Help from a Pigeon

Pinocchio set off for the Fairy's cottage, hoping he would find Geppetto there. Through towns and over fields and meadows, he made his way to the forest where he had first met the Fox and the Cat. But there was no sign of the cottage where it had once stood. In its place was a little marble slab—the Fairy's gravestone.

"Can it be? This must be a mistake," gasped Pinocchio, and he fell to the ground and sobbed.

A pigeon flying overhead saw Pinocchio. The bird flew down and sat beside him.

"I am looking for a puppet named Pinocchio," he said.

"I am Pinocchio!" the puppet replied, surprised.

"Your father, Geppetto, has been looking everywhere for you!" the Pigeon said.

"And I have been looking for him," said Pinocchio. "Where is he now?"

"I left him at the seashore three days ago," said the Pigeon. "He was building a boat so that he could sail across the ocean and search for you in far-off lands."

"How far is it to the seashore?" Pinocchio asked.

"Many, many miles," the Pigeon replied. "If you were walking, it would take you days to get there. But if you hop onto my back, I will fly you there!"

Pinocchio jumped up and settled himself on the Pigeon's back. "Gallop on!" he called out happily, and the Pigeon rose into the air.

Geppetto Is Lost at Sea

Soon the Pigeon was soaring above the clouds. Every time Pinocchio looked down, he got dizzy, so he held tightly onto the Pigeon's neck to keep from falling.

They flew for hours and hours, stopping to rest only once during the night. The next morning, they arrived at the seashore.

Pinocchio was surprised to see a crowd of people standing on the shore, looking out at the sea. Some were shouting and crying, and everyone looked very upset.

"What's wrong?" Pinocchio asked a little old woman.

"There is a man out there," she replied, "in a tiny boat. He made the boat himself, to search for his only son. The water is very rough, and we are afraid the man will drown!"

"That's my father!" Pinocchio cried tearfully. "He's looking for me!"

The waves were tossing the boat around so badly that it kept disappearing. Pinocchio climbed onto a rock and tried to signal to his father. Geppetto must have seen him, because he took off his cap and waved. He tried to turn the boat around and return to the shore.

All at once, a huge wave rose up and overturned his boat. Geppetto was thrown into the dark, raging sea and didn't reappear. The people watching wailed in despair, and some began praying.

"I'll save him!" Pinocchio cried. "I'll save my father!" Bravely, he dived straight into the ocean.

Because Pinocchio was made of wood, it was easy for him to stay afloat, and he swam all day and all night, through rain, hail, lightning, and thunder, until a big wave tossed him up and onto the shore of an island.

At last, the sky cleared, the sun came out, and the sea grew calm once more. Pinocchio looked around for his father's boat, but he couldn't see it anywhere. A dolphin poked its head above the water and greeted him.

"Have you seen a little boat with my father in it?" Pinocchio asked the friendly Dolphin.

"A small boat would have been swamped by the storm last night," the Dolphin replied. "Your father was probably swallowed by the Shark that has been prowling these waters."

"Is the Shark very big?" asked Pinocchio, afraid.

"Big?" said the Dolphin. "Let me put it this way: he is bigger than a five-story building, and his mouth is so deep that a whole train engine could fit in it."

"Oh, no!" cried Pinocchio, more frightened than ever.

No matter how scared of the Shark he was, he had to find Geppetto. First, though, he needed something to eat and drink. The Dolphin told him the way to a nearby village where he might find food, and Pinocchio set off along the road.

A Friend from the Past

As he walked down the hot, dusty road, Pinocchio saw a woman carrying two big jars of water.

"Please," Pinocchio asked, "may I have some water?"

"Of course," said the woman kindly. "You look hungry, too. If you help me carry these water jars home, I will give you something to eat."

Pinocchio agreed, and the woman gave him a wonderful meal of cauliflower with cheese, bread, and cake.

As he was eating, Pinocchio looked up at the woman and realized—could it be? Yes! It was the good, gentle Fairy with Blue Hair! She looked older, but there was no doubt about who she was.

Pinocchio was so happy that he burst into tears.

"I thought you were dead!" he cried. "Oh, how I wish I could grow up just as you have. I wish I were a real boy and you were my mother!"

"You can be a real boy," said the Fairy, "but you have to prove yourself first. You must be kind and obedient and go to school like a real boy. Can you do that?"

"I will, I promise," said Pinocchio. "I want to be a good boy and be a comfort to my father. My poor father! Do you think I'll ever see him again?"

"I am sure of it," said the kind Fairy.

"I am so happy to see you," said Pinocchio. "If only you knew how I suffered when I saw the gravestone…"

"That is why I have come back to you," explained the Fairy. "Your sorrow proved that you have a kind heart."

Trouble at School

Bright and early the next morning, Pinocchio set off for school. He was feeling nervous, but he was determined to study hard and do well, to prove to the Fairy that he deserved to be a real boy.

When he got to school, though, the other boys laughed and made fun of him for being a puppet.

Pinocchio ignored them for as long as he could, but after school they started pulling at his clothes and hitting him. Pinocchio struck back, and soon a big fight broke out.

When people heard all of the shouting and screaming in the street, they called the police, who arrived very quickly—with a big, fierce dog.

All of the boys ran away, and Pinocchio was left alone in the middle of the playground. Afraid of being arrested, he ran toward the sea. The dog ran after him.

Terrified, Pinocchio leaped into the water. The dog jumped in, too, but, strange as it may seem, he couldn't swim! All he could do was bark and pant in fear.

Pinocchio watched him struggle. Then, remembering the Fairy's words and his father's kindness, he grabbed the dog's tail and dragged him to the shore.

The poor dog was so weak that he could barely stand. "Thank you for saving my life, Pinocchio," he gasped, sounding truly grateful.

More Broken Promises

Pinocchio was glad to finally be back on land. After catching his breath and drying himself off, he decided to go back to the kind Fairy's house.

When he got there, she invited him in. Pinocchio told her everything about the teasing by the boys at school and being chased by the big, scary dog.

"I forgive you for fighting with the other boys," she told him. "But you must promise not to get into trouble again."

"I promise," said Pinocchio.

This time, he kept his promise so well that one day the Fairy told him he would get his wish.

"Tomorrow you will become a real boy, and we will have a party to celebrate," she said. "Go invite all of your friends, but be sure to come home before dark."

Pinocchio ran out happily. The first friend he met was a boy named Lampwick. When Pinocchio invited him to his party, Lampwick said he couldn't come.

"I'm going to Toyland," he told Pinocchio. "It's a wonderful place, where you play all day and never have to go to school! You should come, too. The wagon that goes there will be here any minute."

"I promised the Fairy I'd be home before dark," Pinocchio said. Then, after a moment, he asked, "Are you sure there's no school in Toyland?"

"Positive!" said Lampwick.

"Then I will come!" Pinocchio decided.

When the wagon arrived, Pinocchio was happy to see it filled with children of all ages. The driver was a jolly little fat man with a rosy face and the friendliest smile Pinocchio had ever seen. As soon as he saw the driver, Pinocchio knew he was going to have a good time.

Twenty-four donkeys pulled the wagon, and they were all different colors. Some even had blue and yellow stripes! Strangest of all, they wore leather shoes with laces—just like the shoes little boys wear.

It took all night to get to Toyland, and Pinocchio and the others tumbled happily out of the wagon at dawn.

Toyland was different from anywhere Pinocchio had ever seen. There were children shouting and laughing and playing everywhere. Some played ball, others played tag, and others rode bicycles or wooden horses. There were no adults, and nobody looked older than fourteen.

There were no schools and no teachers—no one to shout at the boys or girls or tell them off. The town square was filled with little wooden theaters, and on one wall someone had written:

HURRAH FOR TOYLAND!

DOWN WITH SCHOOL!

"This place is wonderful!" said Pinocchio to Lampwick as they looked around in delight.

"I told you so," Lampwick replied. "Now, let's go play!"

A Nasty Surprise

Five months passed. Pinocchio and Lampwick never opened a book or sat at a desk—they just played and laughed from morning until night, day after day.

Then one morning, Pinocchio had a nasty surprise.

When he woke up, something felt strange. He reached up to touch his head and was shocked to discover that his ears had grown at least ten inches, and they were all hairy!

He rushed to the mirror to look at himself—and discovered that overnight he had grown donkey ears!

He wanted to shout, but all that came out of his mouth was a loud "Hee-haw!" Pinocchio began to weep, and his crying came in little piercing shrieks.

The noise brought Lampwick running into the room. To Pinocchio's horror, Lampwick had grown donkey ears, too!

"What's wrong?" Lampwick tried to say. But he too could manage only a loud "Hee-haw!" When he saw his new ears in the mirror, he began to cry with the same little shrieks as Pinocchio.

The two boys cried until they could cry no more, and then they began to laugh—loud, braying laughs. All at once their arms turned into legs, their faces stretched into snouts, and their backs grew gray, bristly fur. They even grew tails. They had become donkeys!

A knock at the door put a stop to their laughing and braying.

"It's the Wagon Driver," said a voice. "Open up!"

The Wagon Driver smiled at the boys. "You have turned into fine donkeys," he said, gently smoothing their coats. "You are ready to be taken to the market!"

The Wagon Driver was not the kind gentleman he appeared to be. He was a villain who rounded up all of the naughty children who hated school and took them to Toyland. He turned them into donkeys and sold them at the market for the best price he could get.

Lampwick was sold to a farmer, and Pinocchio went to the owner of a circus, who fed him dry straw and taught him to do tricks. When he didn't do his tricks properly, his master beat him. It was a hard life, and Pinocchio was miserable.

"If only I had kept my promises to the kind Fairy," Pinocchio thought glumly, "I would be at home now and so much happier!"

At the circus one night, Pinocchio was supposed to jump through a hoop, but his hind legs got caught and he fell to the floor. When he got up, he was lame.

"You are no use to me anymore," growled his master. The next day, he sold him to a man who wanted to make a drum out of his skin. Pinocchio's new owner then threw him in the sea, waiting for him to drown so that he could skin him. Instead of drowning, Pinocchio swam. And as he swam, his skin fell away; he became Pinocchio the wooden puppet once more.

In the Belly of the Shark

Pinocchio swam happily, relieved to be himself again, when suddenly a horrible sea monster stuck its head out of the water. Its huge mouth was filled with rows of sharp, gleaming teeth, and Pinocchio knew this was the Great Shark. He tried to escape, but he wasn't fast enough. The Great Shark swallowed him whole, and Pinocchio went tumbling down into the monster's belly.

Pinocchio, terrified, tried to feel his way through the Shark's inky black stomach. A kind tuna who had also been swallowed by the Shark was going the other way.

"I am going to try swimming out through the Shark's mouth," said the Tuna. "Come with me."

But Pinocchio was too frightened to follow.

A moment later, he saw a faint light in the distance. As he moved closer, he saw a table set for dinner, lighted by a candle stuck in a bottle. At the table sat a tired-looking old man. Pinocchio almost fainted with happiness when he saw who it was.

"Father!" he cried, running toward the old man.

"Can I believe my eyes?" cried Geppetto, throwing his arms around Pinocchio. "Are you really my own dear Pinocchio?"

"Yes, Father, yes!" said Pinocchio. "And now that I've found you, I will never, ever leave you again."

The two hugged and wept with joy. Then Pinocchio and Geppetto told each other everything that had happened since they had last seen each other.

When they had finished telling their stories, Pinocchio said, "Father, we must find a way to escape. I met a tuna who was going to try swimming out of the Shark's mouth. I think we should try that, too."

"But Pinocchio," said Geppetto, "I can't swim!"

"Don't worry, Father," Pinocchio assured him. "I am a fine swimmer, and I will carry you."

They climbed up the Shark's throat and then waited until the monster was fast asleep.

"The time has come," Pinocchio said to Geppetto. Trying not to slip, they crept across the Shark's huge tongue, right to the opening of its mouth. The old Shark slept with its mouth open, making their task easier.

"Grab my shoulders, Father," Pinocchio whispered. When Geppetto was holding tight, Pinocchio dived straight into the ocean and swam away from the Shark. They were free!

As Pinocchio swam, he could feel Geppetto shivering. He didn't know whether his father was trembling with cold or fear, but he tried to stay calm for both of their sakes.

"It won't be long now, Father," he said. "We must be near the shore."

But they weren't. Pinocchio couldn't see anything but the sea, and he was growing more tired by the minute.

All at once a friendly voice said, "Hang onto my tail. I'll take you to the shore." It was the friendly Tuna that Pinocchio had met in the belly of the Great Shark!

The Tuna brought them safely to the shore. After thanking the fish for saving their lives, Pinocchio and Geppetto walked off in search of a house where they might find something to eat. Geppetto was so weak that he had to lean on Pinocchio's shoulder.

"It's all right, Father," Pinocchio said tenderly. "We can stop whenever you need to rest."

Before they had taken a hundred steps, Pinocchio saw two familiar figures by the side of the road—the Fox and the Cat. They looked miserable! Now the Cat was blind, and the thin, balding Fox had been forced to sell his tail.

"Oh, dear Pinocchio," the Fox said sadly, "please give us a penny or two. You can see how old, tired, and sick we are."

But Pinocchio was not about to be tricked again. He and Geppetto left them by the side of the road.

At the end of the road, they found a tiny straw cottage near a clump of trees. They knocked on the door, and to Pinocchio's amazement, it was answered by…the Talking Cricket!

The Cricket made a warm bed of straw for Geppetto and told Pinocchio about a kind farmer who would give him milk in exchange for help with his chores.

Pinocchio rushed off to the farm, ready to do anything to help his father. He was so happy—for he now knew that the Talking Cricket had been his friend all along.

A Real Boy at Last

Over the next few months, Geppetto grew strong thanks to the milk Pinocchio brought home.

Pinocchio also learned to weave baskets from reeds and sold them at the market. With the money he earned, he bought food and books. He taught himself how to read and studied hard every night.

One night, he fell asleep and dreamed that the Fairy with Blue Hair came to him. "Well done, Pinocchio," she said. "You have shown that you can work hard and that you have a kind heart. I forgive you for all of your past mischief. Keep doing well, and you will be happy."

Pinocchio's eyes flew open, and he found himself in a soft bed in a big, bright room. On a chair was a handsome suit of clothes. When Pinocchio put it on and looked in the mirror, an amazing sight greeted him.

Instead of a puppet looking back at him, there was a rosy-cheeked boy with brown hair and blue eyes!

"Father!" Pinocchio called joyfully. He ran into the next room, and there was Geppetto, carving a beautiful picture frame, just as he used to do. Pinocchio jumped into his father's lap. "Father, look at me!" he said. "I'm not a puppet anymore!"

"No," said Geppetto sincerely. "You are my son, and you have brought me such joy."

"And I am happy, too, Father," said Pinocchio with glee, "now that I am a real boy at last."

About the author

Carlo Collodi's real name was Carlo Lorenzini. He was born in 1826 in Florence, Italy, the oldest of ten children. He worked as a bookseller and a soldier before starting his own newspaper. In 1875, he began writing stories for children, and in 1881, the first chapter of *Pinocchio* appeared in a weekly children's magazine. It was an immediate success, although many people worried that the naughty puppet would set a bad example for children. Carlo died in 1890, unaware of *Pinocchio*'s popularity. He never got married or had children of his own, but his much-loved mischievous puppet lives on to this day.

Other titles in the *Classic Collection* series:

Alice's Adventures in Wonderland • *Little Women*
The Three Musketeers • *Treasure Island*
20,000 Leagues Under the Sea • *Heidi* • *The Wizard of Oz*

Editor: Joanna Pocock • Designer: Andrea Mills
Copyright © QEB Publishing 2012

First published in the United States in 2012 by
QEB Publishing, Inc.
3 Wrigley, Suite A
Irvine, CA 92618

www.qed-publishing.co.uk

A CIP record for this book is available from the Library of Congress.

ISBN 978 1 60992 417 1
Printed in China